eighteen inches

The Distance between the Heart and Mind

Mirtha Michelle Castro Mármol

Andrews McMeel
PUBLISHING®

Other Books by Mirtha Michelle Castro Mármol

Letters, to the Men I Have Loved
Elusive Loves; Amores Esquivos
Letters, to Women Like Me

To the broken,

You are strong.
You are loved.
I wrote this for you.

Warning:

This poetic journal is one woman's vulnerable account of her arduous journey toward self-discovery. Longing to know herself fully— her mind, body, and soul. While reading this book, you may cry, feel nostalgic, or even feel empowered and hopeful. Perhaps you won't see eye to eye with every idea, but it could be you'll see your soul reflected in its pages. You will question things. You will remember your past. You will be thankful for your present. You will dream a new dream. Mostly, you will feel. Welcome to the journey of *Eighteen Inches*, presenting a battlefield between a woman's beat-up heart and her complex mind.

Introduction

When I was a teenager, Daddy was strict. He trusted me, but he didn't trust the people out there—the people I'd eventually meet. Years later, I understood his intentions. He tried to guard me from the world as long as he could. So every time my heart broke into pieces, it was hard to call my daddy. How could I make him feel that he had failed, that the world got to me and he couldn't stop it?

Passionate is an adjective I've always used to describe myself. I am a woman who lives and does everything passionately. When I love, I love hard; when I hurt, I hurt badly. As with everything in our lives, there are consequences when one lives passionately. I was twenty-four years young and riding high on life. My career looked promising, and beauty was on my side, but it was about time my passionate, all-or-nothing nature got me into trouble.

It was a Saturday, and the room was crowded. Somehow there was still more alcohol than people. The eclectic crowd was dancing to the music or taking shots of tequila. Two hours into the party, I saw my ex flirting with another girl and knew I needed to leave immediately, before I did something I would later regret. *I still loved him, and I couldn't show it.* I rushed out of the venue and unapologetically pushed through the crowd. I'm ashamed to admit I was suffering from a bad case of hubris. The friend I came with followed me out and was confronted by a girl whom I had unintentionally bumped into. Both girls had strong personalities, and they quickly turned a nonviolent confrontation into a full-blown physical argument.

Another friend, who saw me rushing to my car, pleaded with me not to drive. Why was I behaving so recklessly? Was I capable of endangering my life and the lives of others because of my selfish need to escape a love triangle? I was stubborn and decided to leave anyway. At the parking garage, I waited for the friend I'd brought to the party. When she got into the car, she was shaken. She told me how the girl I'd bumped into at the party wanted to fight her because she had defended me. I couldn't understand how someone could turn something so miniscule and juvenile into such a dramatic event.

Until then, I knew little about fights or violence outside of watching them on film and television. I had been raised in safe neighborhoods all my life and had been taught that communication can solve many confrontations. That day I received a crude awakening about how malicious and egotistical some people can be. When we attempted to leave the parking garage, we noticed that cars in front of and behind us were at a standstill, and they weren't blocked by other cars. We waited to see what was wrong. Then we noticed it was the same group that was with the girl I had bumped into—they had blocked us in.

My friend began to scream out the window, telling them to move. I tried to control her, pleading with her to be quiet. The other girls became more rowdy. First, one came out of the car in front of us. Then, deaf to my pleas, my friend got out of my car. Another girl came out and headed toward me. Meanwhile, I became really nervous. This was starting to look like something out of my wildest dreams. You know, the dreams where you're being chased by a villain or someone attacks you for no reason, but before anything tragic occurs you make yourself wake up? But there was no waking up here—I was living it, and I had a decision to make. How could I stop this? I lacked experience in many things, and fighting was one of them. Before I could do anything, a fight ensued—three girls against my friend. I got out of the car hoping to break up the fight and "talk it out." What a mistake. Talking things through was clearly not in any of the girls' experience. In those few minutes, I could tell they were most likely all raised completely differently from me. They probably had fights like this before, but I had never thrown a punch. Now I was out of my car and defenseless, while three more girls from the car behind me approached. It turned ugly. No one listened to me, and they started beating up both my friend and me. All I could think of was protecting my face, afraid that it would be scarred. One of the girls pulled my hair viciously and bounced my head against the cement wall. I tried to defend myself and get her off of me, *but all I knew were words.* Too many against us. So I yelled at her and dared her to pull harder because, unlike her hair, mine was real. Another mistake. I had immaturely triggered her, provoking her to grab one of my high heels and smash my head with it. I blacked out.

I woke up in the back seat of my car, confused. I couldn't move from the pain, and I panicked. My hands were bloody. My tanned leather seats were stained red with blood, *my blood.* I touched my thick hair, and it was drenched with my blood. I could hear my friend, who was also bloody and bruised, arguing with two strangers who had helped stop the fight. She was pleading with them to drive us to the nearest hospital because I needed medical attention, but they were afraid to get involved. I leaned forward and looked at myself in the rearview mirror; I screamed. I didn't recognize myself. I touched my face thinking the blood came from a facial wound, but I was wrong. It was worse; I was gushing blood from two open head wounds. Thirty minutes later, I was delirious, crying in an emergency room while nurses stapled my wounds together.

Afterward, as I lay on a cold ER bed, I asked God why such a horrible thing had happened to me? I was simply attempting to stop my friend from getting hurt, and instead, I was the one who ended up terribly injured. I could have died from the head injury, all because I saw something unfair happening, and I couldn't stay put. Many questions ran through my mind that night. Why did I get out of the car? Why was I friends with someone who had such a short temper? Why did I think I was invincible? The next day I had to deal with the police and filing reports. I was furious; I felt violated and vulnerable, and all I wanted was to press charges and make those girls pay for my pain. Two detectives came to my home and took pictures of my wounds and bruises. I felt humiliated as I answered a series of questions that would help them find my attackers. I also had to comfort my worried mother, who felt helpless thousands of miles away. I begged her not to tell my father. I was his pride and joy, and I was afraid the incident would disappoint him and tarnish his opinion of me. Of course, the following day he called. I answered the phone with dread; I knew he already knew. I had to face him and tell him what occurred.

The first words that streamed out of his mouth in Spanish were: "Michelle, what happened? Your mother and sister won't tell me!" I'm not sure where I found the courage to come clean and give him details of the incident. Daddy had a short temper. He grew frustrated and began to yell, *"Eighteen inches, eighteen inches, eighteen inches!"* I had no clue what he meant, and I said, "Daddy, I'm sorry, but I don't understand." Then he said the words that changed my life: "Baby, walk your fingers from your heart to your head; the average distance is eighteen inches.

Every decision you make in your life is based on eighteen inches! You have always been the girl to think only with your heart, but I know you want to be successful, so you must start thinking with your head. You saw your friend in trouble? You shouldn't have gotten out of the car! You should've called 911! Baby, you could have died." His definition of eighteen inches marked me, and since that day, I have tried to find a balance between my heart and mind.

Now, here I am years later after such a horrible episode that I'll never forget. I still have the head scars to prove it happened. But I learned an important lesson. Did I put the eighteen inches advice into practice? Was my passionate nature tamed? Or did I continue down the same road? The answer is here, in *Eighteen Inches*, a book that I waited many years to write. Not because I didn't want to or lacked the inspiration, but because I needed to feel secure in my identity. I needed to deeply know every layer of myself, everything that makes me tick, and everything that triggers my pain and joy. I needed to fully believe that by sharing my most profound vulnerabilities, my discoveries would prove my strength, not weakness. I hope that within these pages the stories of my personal truths will inspire you to observe your own life and understand the power behind your own decisions. I hope these letters and poems will inspire you to dig deeper into your soul and will bring you wonderful insights in the same way they emerged in me.

Genuinely,

Mirtha Michelle Castro Mármol

When I asked for growth
why was I surprised that I was given rain?
When I asked for friendship
why was I torn
when the weeds
were pulled from my flowerbeds?
When I asked for courage
why did I fear
when the day of battle came?
When I asked for love
why did I cry
when I had to face pain?

1"

Mother said I worried her.
She feared I loved too much.
She said,
"It worries me that you'll always feel the need
to be the one who loves more. And there is pain
in that type of love."

Pain

In the past, there were days I'd wake up at dawn and not move for hours. I'd watch the sun rise and ask myself a flood of questions. Those days were usually my worst. At times, I became so engulfed in my sadness that I disappointed myself. I knew better; I was expected to know better. I could do better; I was expected to do better. Those days I felt as if no one understood me. The reality is that I still feel no one actually knows the real me. I've never been an open book with anyone. It's as if I keep 20 percent of my truth to myself, and I give everyone else the rest. Perhaps my mother knows me best, but even she doesn't know all of me. I share many parts of myself with my close friends, but I admit that even the closest don't know all of me. I carry that 20 percent as a secret burden. I am the stranger everyone thinks they know. If they knew my secrets they would judge me. Everyone judges others, even when they say they don't. I release my secrets only in my solitude. I speak them out into the universe, my eternal confidant. Even then there have been times my throat choked up from all the tears, making it impossible to voice those secrets. Still, somehow I've been comforted by the belief that a supreme, loving energy source—the one that created me—listens to me and won't forsake me. Only that knowledge of being loved by God has saved me from my most complex thoughts. That belief has saved me from wondering what would happen if I were to cut my wrist or drive off a cliff. Yes, I've had suicidal thoughts, and I'm no longer ashamed to speak about past pain. At times it was unbearable, and I wondered who would mourn me if I were gone. Who would miss me? Because my desire to be loved is stronger than the wall I built around myself. I ultimately put a stop to those fearful thoughts—my desire to be loved runs deep, but my love for my loved ones runs even deeper. I've learned that's what I know how to do best . . . *I love*. I am talented at loving people.

From the outside, I am a beam of light. Most days I am happy and grateful. Then I'm the life of the party. I make jokes, give away hugs and smiles. Do you know how important hugs are? Sometimes I wish for a sincere hug. The type of hug that adjusts your spine—one that transmits a selfless love. Sadly, I've gone weeks and even months without an energy exchange like that, which always makes me miss my family because my nephew hugs me that way. I smother him in return because I want him to feel my love. I want him to know that he is loved. When you have that amount of love around you, you might take it for granted. I've taken many hugs for granted. I've taken much love for granted. When there is abundance, one rarely thinks about what a life of emptiness would be like. The rich man hardly thinks of how life would be as a poor man. The healthy man hardly thinks of how life would be as a sick man. It's hard to fully understand how others feel until life hands us the same cards, until we walk in someone else's shoes. Our fate of emptiness or abundance isn't always decided by our decisions. Sometimes our place of birth has greater influence on what our lives become, but I've learned that regardless of the latitude and longitude of where we are born, we all have the ability to choose love.

On the days I feel pain, it envelopes me and almost destroys me. I understand that I'm not the only one secretly holding on to pain. We are often ignorant of what others are experiencing because of the common fear about voicing our feelings. Have you ever hugged someone only to have them burst into tears, had someone's vulnerability melt in your arms? I have, and it has broken my heart to feel someone else's pain. We are all hurt people walking through life carrying pain within us without the knowledge of how to heal. Many are afraid to be vulnerable with others because that can open the door for more pain, and at times, it is considered to be weakness. In truth, to be vulnerable is a gift.

Meanwhile, there are some who are able to block the pain from their memory, some live with it like a crutch, and others let it coexist with love. Pain and love are much like darkness and light. I am grateful for the moments of darkness because only then can I see the light that bursts in. In the same way *I understand that pain has polished me and reminded me of my need for love.*

The desire to be understood
is always rooted in the desire to be loved.

The desire to be loved
is rooted in the desire to be accepted.

When will I stop seeking desires
and begin to recognize that
no one will love me more than I can?

No one will understand my inner havoc
more than I can.

Why do I seek in humans
what already exists inside me?

Because the world lied to me, and I believed it.

I guard my pain
the way I guard my happiness.
I keep it alive in me,
pumping in my rib cage.

Why?
Because it reminds me of the times
I burned in the fire,
but was strong enough
to rise from the ashes.

And if I must burn again,
I shall continue to rise,
and from the ashes be reborn,
again and again.

To rise from the ashes

I don't expect people to understand me anymore.
My mind has been stretched far too wide.
Love has made me understand
that I don't need to be understood
to possess the ability to understand others.

When I developed empathy

To grow too inward,
to grow too profound
in the root,
is where the plant's survival lies.

The effects of my solitude

My heart is heavy,
screaming in silence.
A volcano
waiting to erupt.
Maybe I need to burst
into an explosion of tears.

Have I forgotten how to cry?

Pain is like the rain,
it arrives eventually.

After a drought,
it will flood.

The rain cleanses.
The rain nourishes.

We need the rain,
just like pain.

The climate of pain

I tell myself I must bare my soul
in order to be understood.
I must give intricate details
to explain who I am.
If only my mother had taught me.
The flower doesn't explain
why she has petals.
The flower simply blooms
according to her nature.
Mother, I don't blame you,
you're a vulnerable artist too.

The things I tell myself

I expect the sun to rise,
but how dare I expect reciprocity?
I expect the tree to bear fruit,
but how dare I expect our bond to mature?
I expect the weather to change,
but how dare I expect a different behavior
    from you?
I expect rainbows after the rain,
and solar eclipses
when the moon blocks the sun,
but how dare I expect sincere love?
The paradox of human nature is that
we teach each other to expect
supernatural miracles.
Yet, when it comes to human relations,
we teach each other
to have no expectations.

The paradox of human nature

2"

When you're young, you think you will meet many people who will spark a fire within you. You think that chemistry is easy to come by. And so there will be people you will take for granted. Then one day you'll realize how special and rare those people were. You'll find yourself reminiscing about the exact feeling they gave you, and in my case, chasing it.

Destiny

Running into him is painful, especially when he's with her. If only she knew what having *him*—the man who was once my everything—around me feels like. I saw the way he looked at me. There was a certain fear in his aura, as his eyes secretly found their way to mine. How can just saying hello and touching him for seconds leave such a mark in my memory? Within seconds, I felt the soft texture of his hair, his scent penetrated my senses, and once more, I breathed him fully. Why is it that years after our abrupt ending, this feeling is still hard to let go of? How is it that the heart can still feed off an old love? But who am I to place a time limit on love? Time is nonexistent when it comes to love.

When our eyes meet and others aren't watching, we both know the flame that once burned between us is still there. If the eyes indeed are the windows to our soul, then he is the one who sees my naked soul. When his eyes connect with mine, they confirm what I've always known: our souls have encountered each other many times before. This lifetime was unfair to us, and we didn't get it right. Maybe I met him when I was too young or maybe too hurt. Maybe I wasn't wise enough to recognize he was more than just a lover; *he was true love.*

When I see him with her, I can't help but think she resembles me. Did he seek me in her? Do her eyes ever connect to his soul like mine did? I don't mean to be disrespectful, but when I remember us then, our out-of-this-world passion was undeniable. We were fire—how can he ever live without that fire again? How have I lived without that same fervor? How is it that we felt such a connection, and destiny still didn't decide in our favor? Does it mean that we must live out another story, hoping for a better outcome? Or must we simply rely on the delusion that we'll meet in another lifetime and get it right then? It is as if the idea of what we could have been is more powerful than the reality of what we became. I've told myself many times that it wasn't about bad timing, and that our current reality was our destiny, a destiny I must accept. Yet, silently I have also told myself that maybe destiny is an excuse for cowards who didn't fight enough for what they deeply wanted. In our story, we were both cowards, beginning with me.

Sometimes I want to reach out. Sometimes I imagine him approaching me, like dark dreams that live in light. Sometimes I wish I had been wiser and braver with him. Sometimes I wish I had never sacrificed my heart for pride, and now my nights wouldn't be lonely. On the contrary, they would be filled with him and his contagious laugh. Once again, I understand that it's too late, and I must live with the fact that he moved on, perhaps not knowing how deeply I loved him. He'll never know that our first kiss was what made me believe in soul mates. That before him, chemistry was only a subject. Such a strong connection can't ever be denied or forgotten. Meanwhile, I travel through cities meeting new souls, living out adventures, and diving into new experiences, but still comparing what I felt with him to how I want to feel again.

I have to be careful
about missing the life
I never had
with someone I lost.

Let go.

If I could have him again
I would write him love letters
while he is still
next to me.
I would give them to him
after sealing them with my kiss.
If he were to leave
I'd have peace of mind
in knowing that he knows
exactly how my heart beats for him.
How his scent
erupts all lost passions in me.
How my heart will always
have a vacancy for him.

The hope in wishing

What is sorrow?
Sorrow is knowing he is right there,
right in front of me,
and I can't reach out and touch him.

How lost love feels

Maybe I never said
what my smile shouted out.
Maybe I never said
how breathless you made me feel.
Maybe it was always enough
as long as you touched me.
Regardless,
one truth I know.
When our eyes met,
I recognized your soul.

This truth I know.

There will be days in the spring
when life will not bloom
but will stay centered at its root.

Much like his breath,
invisibly coexisting alongside mine,
that must be consumed.

Because my atoms still attract his
even when our chemistry
became the subject
of a failed love story
within pages of a book.

Lovers, we are forced to live
a million minutes
without each other,
a million breaths
without our lungs.

And if our largest organ is our skin,
explain to me
how will I continue to live without his touch?

When I was forced to accept destiny

My heart feels heavy.
There are a thousand silent bricks weighing
    it down
with my yearning.
It is my soul yearning for him.
At times I feel a magnetic pull toward him,
wherever in the world he might be.
It is my soul dancing toward him.

I imagine his face,
just as it was the last time I saw him.
I can trace every feature and line.
A tear trickles from my right eye.
While in my transient state—
I wonder can he feel me thinking of him?
I wonder can he feel me feeling him?

The unexplainable science of missing
someone's energy

Don't get me wrong,
I have loved after you.
I have loved faithfully
and deeply.
All of those other loves
I keep them guarded.
Some in the vaults of my memory
and some within the walls of my heart.
I must admit some have been special,
but none of their memories
has the power to keep me up at night.
None of their eyes
can haunt me at dawn.
The night and its trickery
are like fog blinding the eye.
Yet it never ceases to fool me
because in the end tears fill my eyes.

All because you are not with me

Friends who got their happy ending
tell me I need to let him go.
They tell me to move on.
Don't they understand?
When true love is experienced
you can suppress it in silence
or tuck it away as a memory.
But it never goes away.

A love too deep

I always knew we wouldn't last.
I always knew I'd watch you
marry someone else.
I always had a heavy feeling,
especially when I looked into your eyes.
If only I knew then what I know now,
but youth is blinding
and the ego conniving.
With a heart full of anger,
with a heart full of passion,
I've searched for you in many others,
and I have never found you.

When I'm nostalgic

You give playing with fire
a dangerous new meaning.
It no longer means the possibility
of being caught by the flames of lust.
It no longer means the breathlessness
caused by too much heat.
It has gone beyond the limits of passion,
and now the attachment consumes my soul.

You are my voiceless attachment.

God knows, not everyone has the capability
of understanding lost love.
Could you imagine if *everyone*
had the strength to withstand
being torn apart in half,
and the body parts
somehow managing to survive?

No, I cannot.

3"

The past is not the past
if it continues to live with you.

Brave

Acting classes were always cathartic for me. I considered them to be a powerful way of connecting strangers through a journey of emotions. At age twenty-five, I experienced such a journey during a scene study class that forced me to come to terms with an incident from my past. At the beginning of each class, the coach handed all the students a scene to prepare, and we would later have to perform it in front of the class. The goal of the session was to break down every wall and practice the art of being. It was our objective as thespians to become the assigned character and express the complete honesty the scene required. On that particular day, as I read the scene I was scheduled to perform, I found it far too familiar. The female character met a male character with the name of someone I had known in my past. She met him in a similar fashion, and after a date, she ended up like me, with her hands forced against a bed, raped at twenty years old. In this case, art imitated life, and the blocked memory of that awful night surged into my present. We often underestimate how fragile the mind can be. That evening, I was forced to act out my own truth—one I had hidden for years from everyone in my life. *All because of shame.*

My upbringing was conservative. I wasn't perfect in any way, but I had a strong set of values that I always stood by, especially when I had to make decisions. I was a girl who wanted experience, but I didn't color much outside the lines. I was twenty when I met him through a mutual friend who knew him from the Ivy League university they had both attended. He was twenty-three and appeared to be a sweet guy. He contacted me, and I accepted his invitation to the movies. After the show, we grabbed a bite, and I went home. Everything about him seemed normal. Days later, on a Friday night, I agreed to go with him to a party hosted by one of his neighbors. I always loved the idea of meeting new people, and I understood how important new experiences were for growth. I met him at his apartment, and we walked over to the party together. The gathering felt a lot like a college frat party. Everyone was drinking, and I didn't shy away from joining them. The hours flew by, and I knew it was time for me to go home. He said I shouldn't go home just yet because it was a long drive back to the suburbs, and I had drunk enough to get pulled over. I agreed to stay at his apartment until I sobered up. I figured an hour was all I needed before I could head back home. That was when my naivete got me into trouble. He gave me some water, and as I sat on his couch, he told me I could lie down on his bed until I had to go. I agreed. He said I could get comfortable. After about twenty minutes, he walked into the room and lay down next to me. At first it was innocent. He kissed me. *I kissed him back.* Then he started caressing my arms, and his hands began to travel down to my thighs. I started to feel uncomfortable. Then he tried to run his fingers around my private parts. I moved his hands away. I had just lost my virginity the year before, but there wasn't a promiscuous bone in my body. He began to get aggressive. I wanted to leave. When I got up, he said, "Sorry, I'll stop. I'll go to the couch." That moment changed everything. I believed him. I should have left and sobered up in my car. Unfortunately, back then I was gullible, and although I had read about rape, I never thought it would ever happen to me. He got up and walked away as I lay back down. Minutes later, he came back to the bed and started to caress me again, but this time he didn't stop. He was tall and strong and had an athletic build. He pressed

my arms back, and although I tried, I wasn't strong enough
to push him back. "Stop!" I yelled repeatedly. As I pleaded
with him to stop, he held my arms down, pushed up my skirt,
aggressively pulled down my panties, and forced my legs open.
I screamed *No!* but fear came over me, and I gave up, knowing
that eventually it would end. Being sober didn't matter—all I
wanted to do was leave in one piece. He pressed me down and,
without looking at me, viciously thrust into me. He was like a
man possessed, without any self-control, and his ears were deaf
to my pleading. Minutes felt like an eternity, with my playing
a broken record in my head, "It will end, it will end, it will
end . . ." The ceiling witnessed my numbness, and my eyes filled
with water. Sometimes a single tear can carry more pain than
an entire broken dam. When he was finished, I immediately
got up, pulled down my skirt and left the apartment. I ran out
of the building in a hurry and got in my car. A cloud of shame
enveloped me, and I burst into tears.

The first thing I did was blame myself. I told myself
I shouldn't have worn that short skirt. I blamed myself for
trusting someone I hardly knew. I felt dirty. I felt violated. What
I didn't realize was that it wasn't my fault. I didn't do anything
to deserve what happened to me. No one deserves to be pinned
down and abused. Society has always made female victims feel
they were partly to blame for their rapists' attacks. It's simple:
no means no. I arrived back home and immediately showered.
I remember sitting on the shower floor and crying hysterically.
I felt worthless, tainted, and disrespected. The water wasn't
enough to wash off what had occurred that night.

The next day he tried to reach out, but I did not pick up
any of his calls. For days he left me voicemail after voicemail
saying he was sorry, but without fully recognizing what he had

done to me. He probably didn't mean the apology, but he was afraid of what I'd do. Afraid of getting in trouble with his rich parents or the law. Date rape is by far more common than most people think. I wasn't beaten and left half-dead in a desolate alley as some women have been; I was raped by someone who didn't *seem* like a rapist. I wondered if he had raped other girls before. The ease with which he did it made me think he had, and he'd gotten away with it. From that day on, I avoided any place I thought he might be out of fear of meeting him and revisiting what had happened. I never saw him again, but I will always be haunted by his face and the way he violated my mind, body, and spirit.

After that, I didn't trust men's appearances, and I lost trust in all of them. The next man I allowed into my life was the complete opposite of my previous preppy preferences. He was very different from an Ivy League college graduate. His appearance might have classified him as trouble, but he was gentle, and most importantly, never forced me to do anything I wasn't ready for. Sadly, I learned the hard way that sometimes we immediately judge a book by its cover, as I had for years. I never allowed the rape incident to take the essence of my soul, and I refused to be categorized as a victim. But years later during that acting class, I learned that my wound was far from healed because I never gave it the proper attention.

It was unbearable for me to perform the dreadful scene my coach had unknowingly chosen for me, like throwing salt on that wound. She sensed something was wrong and asked me about it. It was unlike me to forget my lines or experience stage fright, but I couldn't hold it in, and I burst into tears. I had bottled up the emotions of that night far too long. I had kept it hidden within me because of the shame that I never did anything about the rape. I never filed a police report, and by not doing so, I left other women at risk. I never told my parents for fear of disappointing them. I never told anyone because I felt disgusted with myself, when I should only have felt disgusted by my rapist. On that stage, I cried out all those fears, and eventually, I regained my voice. I let go of the notion that speaking out about an abuse done to me was a form of self-pity. That night, my coach hugged me and said I was brave for sharing my experience. Truthfully, I can't say I felt brave, but I can say I was one step closer to it. I went home to my boyfriend at the time and told him what happened in class. I needed to come clean with what I had been holding in, knowing that experience had affected my trust in relationships with men. He hugged me, and I allowed myself to feel safe for the first time. I knew I had the right to always feel safe.

Years later, after the release of my first book, many young women wrote to me seeking advice on overcoming pain. From the different letters I received, the stories of rape struck the deepest chord with me. Some dealt with feelings of worthlessness and even disrespect for their own bodies as a result. It's so much easier to view sex as casual and less meaningful after being raped. Rape can be much like slavery. One doesn't have to be chained physically to remain enslaved mentally. Reading those letters helped me understand that the most important step I could take toward properly healing was sharing my story. I wrote back to all those who sent letters, assuring them their worth was not determined by the abuse they endured. They still had their power, and within that power they had the choice to forgive and let go. There is freedom in forgiveness. Taking the steps to forgive those who hurt us is necessary in order to be liberated from emotional trauma.

It took some time, but I learned that how I view and care for myself is in my own hands. Learning to trust again is also in my hands, and so is healing. It was a personal decision to put the experience behind me, and I understood that my story deserved my own voice. Courage isn't learned by reading books. We can only read about examples of courage. We find courage when we make the decision to confront our fears and our shame. *The decision to face my shame is what eventually made me brave.*

When I inhaled you,
it never crossed my mind
that exhaling you
would be so painful.

My emancipation

The idea of unrealized love is romantic.
Have you thought that it's possible to fall in
love with the idea of someone
and not with their reality?

Maybe, I'm afraid that you will not fall in
love with the real me,
all the shades of me—everything that makes
the reality of me.

Maybe, it's all rooted in my fear that the
idea of me is far more attractive,
a big box decorated with a big red bow—the
inside unknown.

Maybe, my fears stem from my pain.
Have I only been loved from afar, and
never up close?

I understand.
Not everyone can cope with the sight of blood.

It takes about three weeks
for a flesh wound to heal.

What about the heart?
How long does it take?

Broken hearts have questions too.

When women were labeled fragile,
it wasn't synonymous with weakness.
It came from the understanding that
they had the power
of discerning how fragile trust can be.
Once trust is broken
they can also break.
Tell me, if we repair our trust
will time's passage smooth out
the rough ridges of my breakage, too?

The fragility of trust

4"

To the emotionally damaged:
don't let the strength you built
block your heart from the ability to love.

Pride

It took me years and countless mistakes to understand that I've lost more than I've gained by holding on to pride. How often have I lost out on love because of my pride? How often have I missed out on an incredible opportunity—all because of my pride? Rules I created for myself at an early age and my cultural programming and conditioning certainly were root causes of the pride I developed throughout my life. Pride is stubborn; it sets roots into your heart, causing damage along the way.

I grew up thinking "the boy" is supposed to chase "the girl." She is supposed to play hard to get, to be special in his eyes. Worse, the girl is a princess, and the boy is a prince who has to rescue her. Even worse, the princess has to wait until the frog becomes a prince and for him to finally realize she is insanely special. The most naive thought I've ever had was believing I was a princess in need of saving. Princes don't save; only love saves—and I was simply a human being in need of love, not understanding that all the love I craved was already inside me. Still, as I waited for a happily ever after, I lost out on multiple opportunities that could have been great for me. Sometimes I think waiting is another word used to mask fear. Those who don't wait and go after what they want are considered fearless. They are visionary souls who may lack wisdom but possess courage. I admit many times I have lacked both.

In the past, I have allowed pride to consume me and tarnish my relationships. I have also been too jaded to allow myself the space to be vulnerable. Fear has impeded me from reaching new heights in love because the idea of rejection lingered, far too potent. With the man I loved, I allowed sexual intimacy to have more power than telling him how much I loved him. As if my flesh could ever speak the words my soul was made to say. What I didn't realize was that men can become jaded as well, and sometimes, simple words of validation can dispel their feelings, and even inspire them to admit their own vulnerability. When I was young and inexperienced, I thought I had to play a game to keep him. You know, the game your young, immature, single girlfriends advise you to play? The one that involves not returning phone calls right away, while you are counting the hours and minutes and don't decide to call back until you are practically delirious. The game that suggests you should act like a *bitch* because, according to a popular book, men love bitches. Because of this game, I became a victim, and I got played instead of playing myself.

After the games are done, there are only regrets left. It's politically correct for me to say that I don't believe in regrets because I'm the lover type who believes in destiny. What was meant to be was what I eventually had to live. I'll never regret the stories I've lived, but I have regretted my behavior and having too much pride. I regret not being vocal enough when I had the chance to speak out. I regret waiting for the *right moment* and then seeing what or whom I wanted pass by right in front of my eyes. I regret not being vulnerable and then wondering what would have happened if I had been. How proactive must I be in order to bring about the changes that I yearn for? How much of my pride should I put aside?

I began reflecting on what perfect love is—the unconditional love many humans strive for, but often fail to achieve. Practicing that type of unconditional love every day is far from easy. Human connections introduce us to a world of love and pain. Sometimes the damage is immediately visible, and we must constantly look within to see which areas need healing. Through pain and heartbreak I found strength, but eventually I asked myself: Is my strength only adding more to my existing pride? It's the quintessential tug-of-war. My strength became a trait I valued, but I didn't realize I was creating more pride within me. I saw my silence as strength, but within my silence there was pain rooted in pride, and that pride was rooted in fear. It was the fear of not being accepted or loved if those whom I loved discovered my flaws. Now I understand that proper healing doesn't reflect pride, and perfect love doesn't embody fear. Imagine if the creator told his creation, "I love you, but my pride didn't let me show it." How disappointing and painful would that be? Thankfully, the creator embodies perfect love, so he'd never say that to his creation. Yet how many times have I said it to people I love? How many times have I fallen short in love because of my pride? It's been hard to knock down the walls I myself built out of fear because of my need to protect my heart. If I choose to let love in, it comes at a price. I can't experience love if I don't allow people in. Every day I must take the chance and sacrifice my ego. *I must consciously make the decision to surrender and peel away the layers my pride built in the hope of understanding and experiencing perfect love.*

He told me I was strong.
If only he knew I was broken glass
and was a finger flick away
from having all my glued pieces
shattered once again.

Broken glass

What is it with us humans?
We must first experience loss
in order to understand love.

And I thought I was mature.

My problem wasn't letting go,
I knew I could surrender.
My problem was that I held on stronger
than yesterday and the day before.

I was born stubborn.

To find the root
of our fears
we must first
look in the mirror.

The work starts within.

As a child I learned
that the higher you climb,
the harder the fall.
That explains
why falling in love
with you is easy.
But also why I'm afraid
to let go
and risk it all.

Without risk, there is no reward.

4"

I've accepted the fact
that we are
no longer *"We."*
We are now a pair of *"I"*s

And that hurts.

I am mad at you!
How dare you run away?
I am angry at you!
Don't you see how high we could have flown?
Now I'm at a loss for words.
All I can do is remember our last embrace
And wonder why you were too scared to stay.
I am tremendously disappointed!
How dare you teach me about this feeling
then selfishly take it all away?

How dare you?

It's amusing when I'm told
that what I need
is only a want.
And what I want
is not a need.

As if they knew
what type of blood
my body needs.

I thought I had time.
I thought you'd always be there.
But time waits for no one.
Why did I expect
that you and time would be any different?

People can choose not to wait at all.

5″

I want to live without the human
perception of time.

Death

Her name was Ana Rosa, and saying her name out loud still brings tears to my eyes. She had golden-almond skin and yellowish eyes. She wore her hair short and always wore mid-calf skirts; never much makeup except powder and always had her reading glasses nearby. She was of British ancestry, so her last name was always mispronounced in my native Spanish tongue. It was Lightbourn, and, indeed, every time she walked into a room, light would shine through her. She was a person filled with selfless love and contagious joy. She had discipline, and she took on tasks others wouldn't touch. She was generous and gave the clothes off her back if she saw someone in need. She never married and was childless, and it seems as if she knew that was her fate. Little did she know destiny had a child in store for her.

My grandmother met her at church in the late '60s, and soon after, they became best friends. As a result, she considered my grandmother's children to be her family. She became a fixture in my grandparents' household, and because she didn't have a spouse or children, my grandparents included her in almost everything we did as a family. Decades into their friendship, when my mother was pregnant with me, my mother expressed the need for extra help. She was a working mom finishing her university studies. Ana Rosa stepped up to the plate and said she'd be my nanny.

I wish I could remember the first time she held me, so I could see her first reaction. Did she recognize me? Did she feel an immediate connection? She always said that when I was born she squeezed my cheeks, and that formed my dimples. I believed that story my entire childhood. I'd even tell her that she didn't squeeze hard enough on the cheek with my half dimple. She'd reply that she loved me so much, and she was afraid to squeeze too hard and hurt me because I was a small baby. She called me Nuna, and I called her Nana, and the bond that grew between us was evident. My mother admitted there were times she felt jealous and worried that I loved Ana Rosa more than her. I undoubtedly loved my mother deeply, but it was difficult to explain what I intuitively felt for my Nana. I felt an immense love for her and from her. I felt she was the only person I never had to share. It's as if I knew our souls were deeply connected. People often refer to soul mates as romantic partners, but I've learned soul mates aren't only lovers. They can also be friends and family. It is an instant connection that time doesn't easily break. You feel a comfort between you immediately. When your eyes first meet, there is an unexplainable pull because you recognize each other. Each of us can have a large soul family and meet in different lifetimes in different roles. It all depends on what we are meant to learn in that lifetime in order to evolve our soul.

When I was five, my parents decided to move the family to Miami, Florida. I know she was heartbroken, as was I. I was only a child and couldn't understand why she couldn't come with us. I was upset and hurt. Who would ever love me as much as she? I knew I was her everything. I was being ripped away from everything I knew, and I had no say in the decision. People think children can easily adapt and won't be as affected by change, yet why is it that I remember it all? I remember those last months, telling her that I loved her and would never forget her. My parents comforted me, saying I'd spend every summer back in the Dominican Republic. Indeed, every year came around, and

I would be with my family and my Nana. Those summers were glorious, full of laughter and love. Water balloon fights, playing baseball till late hours, going to the beach, and eating the best fried fish under the sun. My Nana was always by my side. She made me my favorite meals, bathed me, and always knew what I wanted before I did. At the end of the day, memories are all we have. We become a collection of our memories. The years flew by, and during the summer after my high school graduation, tragedy struck. I had a dream in which I saw her young and glamorous. In the dream I admired how beautiful she looked, and I said goodbye to her. I awoke sobbing. I feared I knew what the dream meant—death was near.

I called her frantically, and she said she was OK. She always hid her medical conditions. Never the attention seeker, she always took the selfless role. I confided the dream to my grandmother, and I pleaded for no one to lie to me. She later confessed that Ana Rosa had not been well but had refused to worry anyone. When I visited that summer, I found the courage to tell her about my dream. I cried helplessly as she hugged me and said, "Maybe that means I'm getting ready to be with the Lord." I refused to accept her answer. I told her that she was wrong. She had many more years to live—after all, she had yet to meet my future children. I had the same attachment to her at seventeen as I did when I was a child. A mother isn't only the woman who gives birth; she is someone who nurtures, who loves, who raises the child—and she was a mother to me.

Three months after the fateful dream, on August 2, 2001, my Nana passed. She suffered a brain hemorrhage, and although I was able to express my last words to her in a letter, I still carry her loss with me like a stubborn ache in my throat. She is the tear in my eye that never dries. Our souls can carry many painful memories that are difficult to completely let go of. When she passed, I felt it was a story cut short too soon. An unfinished poem that I'm still trying to write the ending to, and all I can come up with are questions. How does a mortal accept the death of a loved one without losing our own soul in the process? How can we become entwined with another soul and expect life to be the same without it? How can I leave the pain behind without forgetting her? How can the joy of our memories give me solace for the years to come without her?

There are times when I ponder what her dreams were and if she felt fulfilled. I also think of the role I played in her life, and she in mine. Love always comes to mind. In the infinite cycle of life, love is its origin. Love is the God particle in all of us. Love is what bonds us. It is love that survives death and goes beyond the chambers of this world we attach ourselves to. Her purpose in my life and mine in hers was to experience what it is like to be loved selflessly. There are many moments when I feel her presence. Her energy caresses me and gives me comfort when I most need it. It's as if she sees my pains and my struggles and stays by my side. Many times I see her in my dreams, and in them she guides me to the right doors to open. I'll never know how real the dreams are, or if my subconscious is playing tricks on me, but it always feels peaceful. I don't need a scientific explanation for what I feel. It is my personal belief that when my day comes, I'll be face to face with the mysteries of the universe. Until then, I understand physical death is not the end, and I've learned not to be afraid of it. There is a lesson in everything that is lived and in everything that is lost. Sometimes the lesson is greater when it involves people we love. When I lost my Nana, I was challenged to seek a deeper understanding of death, and it led

5"

me to finding her alive in everything I do. Alive in the things she taught me, alive in the stories she shared with me, alive in the parts of her she left me. *She lives in my heart, in my words, and now in these pages.*

Sometimes I miss certain people.
I see their names written on random places,
or I hear a song that's part of a memory.
It's like my mind wants to
keep them alive in me,
or the universe wants
to play a haunting game.
Maybe they are still with me,
and there are invisible strings between us.

The ghosts that surround me

5″

There are no words to console
a heart mourning a loved one.
There is no color to paint
the dark shadow of death.
There is no breeze to calm
the grief of a goodbye.
There aren't enough hands
to wipe away aching tears.
There are only feelings left
that boil to the surface.
Feelings too large
for hugs to bear.
Feelings too painful
for a throat to withstand.
Yet with passing time,
silence and its emptiness
will fill the vacant room of grief,
especially when memories
bring forth echoes of the past.

When I saw my mother grieve for her mother

Eighteen Inches

It was the summer of '94
when I learned about a woman
who changed the history
of the country in which I was born.
I saw her face painted
on a monument by the *Malecón*.
It haunted me for days
until I asked about her.
My Nana always said
she was brave,
she fought for human rights
then was murdered
for standing up for what was right.
For some she was a legend,
the victim of a ruthless tyrant.
I read about her life
and her struggle to witness our nation's freedom.
No, she wasn't a slave—
she was simply born at the wrong time
and of the wrong sex.
Described as a beauty in her day,
her true beauty was in her mind.
She possessed a restless nature,
a revolutionary at heart.
Her name was Minerva,
like the Roman goddess of wisdom.
Her name was Minerva,
my tongue knows her name.
Her story bravely lives on
long beyond her fate.

Legends never die

Forever
is a dangerous word.
How can a mortal
offer eternity?

In the end we are souls
drifting
until we find a home.
And when I found you
it was difficult
to leave you.

Love is our home.

6"

We all need healing.
The mistake is to believe that we don't.

Experience

The Japanese treat broken pottery differently from most other cultures. I was taught to dispose of a piece of ceramic once it shatters. Instead, the Japanese take the broken pieces and create art from them. They lacquer the broken pieces with gold and silver finish, proudly showcasing their broken history. They call this the art of *kintsugi*. Isn't it ironic that our broken past can sometimes bring out the most beautiful parts of us? And isn't it somber that we are told scars bring shame instead of gratitude for surviving the fall?

I experienced a terrible burn on my index finger. I tried to stop a small fire in my apartment when a large amount of tissue paper from a package caught the wrath of a burning candle. For a moment, I was clueless about what to do. I had never had to stop a fire. I picked up the burning balls of tissue so nothing else on the table would also catch fire. Thankfully, a friend who was visiting ran to the kitchen for a pot of water. She threw it at me, and the worst part was over. Then she went back for more water to put out the remaining flames. It was a frightening experience. I can go on and on about how I felt protected in that moment, but the enlightenment came after, when my burn began to heal. I was surprised to see that only one finger had burned badly because both hands had been pretty much in flames. I began to observe the healing process of the burn, trying to understand the importance of each stage.

At first there was a terrible sting and pain, then blisters, and my skin changed colors from a light pink to purple, then to a dark brown scab. There was continuing discomfort, and many times I felt grateful that my entire hand didn't burn. I was also grateful to my friend for helping me stop the fire. I began to compare the burn experience to others in my life, including heartbreak. Many times I have used the expression "burned by love," but interestingly enough, I had never experienced a real burn. My imagination and empathy for others who seemed badly burned made me feel I already understood the discomfort, but I was wrong. It's always different when one personally experiences the ordeal. The same occurred when I first experienced heartbreak. The bigger the heartbreak I experienced, the more I was able to understand myself and others. I began to understand that enlightenment occurs when one navigates through the many stages of pain. We must first burn in order to grow new skin, a much tougher skin. We must first lose in order to value progress.

I have often asked my creator for the opportunity to reach new levels—a new stage in my life—without realizing that to reach a new height I must first shed the previous level, the old skin. Only the experience gained by burning different stages can prepare me for my next skin. Throughout the many healing stages of my life, I have encountered certain personal truths. These are the beliefs that define me today—how I treat and how I react to others. How I cope with loss and failure. How to be courageous. How to walk in love and disarm hate. To gain experience one must first live everything, and *I am not afraid to burn to ashes because only from nothing can I become again.*

6"

The fear that someone
other than you
can love whom you love
much better than you.

Too many adults being ruled by
childish insecurities

My flaws are part of me.
My scars are part of me.
My mistakes are part of me.
My pains are part of me.

As is my love!
As is my success!
As is my beauty!
As is my joy!

Why define my essence by one star
when there is *an entire universe*
already burning
and shining within me!

When I realized how bright I was

I've learned love is kind.
Love is selfless.
But when I chose to love myself first
I was told I was selfish.

What I learned about love

Eighteen Inches

A rose
isn't ashamed
of its thorns.
So why should I be
ashamed of my mistakes?

When I accepted my thorns

Why did I choose to let go?

I became tired
of fixing people
who were constantly
breaking me.

7"

Most people see only the physical world,
then wonder why their dreams never come true.
Wonderful experiences require supernatural faith.

Faith

Most religions tend to be full of rules and constraints, and that has resulted in the spread of divisiveness and separatism among many groups. After all, religion is a man-made institution with the purpose of controlling different groups. When I think of what religion has done to the world, I become embarrassed and enraged. How can something as beautiful and pure as proclaiming faith in an all-loving God, a supreme energy source, be corrupted and demoralized into a weapon of soul destruction—simply because of greed, ego, and power? Hateful crimes have been performed throughout the centuries in the name of God. I've always wondered who is this God who inspires such hate? When I think of the higher power I have placed my faith in, I think of unconditional love, not fear. My God heals; he doesn't break me. My God doesn't divide; he restores. My God is *love*. I am able to navigate through life with hope because of his love for me. Many times I have been tested. Sometimes I feel I am tested more than others because I am a woman of faith. I've been dragged through the mud, and I've been broken on different occasions. Yet I still allow myself to believe the best is yet to come, that I was given hope and a future for a purpose much larger than myself.

When I was tested, I felt my life was about to crumble. I have experienced setback after setback, and many times the future seemed hazy. Those were the times when I expected to fail, to drown in worry, but my faith restored me. I've learned to go into deep solitude and talk to my creator. I share my feelings and my worries—how I need strength and help to see clearly. I give thanks and praise in the midst of the storm; the noise does eventually become quiet, and peace arrives. I am always grateful for the storm because it brings me closer to him. Through the storm, I have formed an intimate relationship with my creator. I have witnessed miracles along the way—episodes that some people might consider coincidences were actually his hand working in my favor.

I believe that we're all spiritual beings having a physical experience on Earth. Once our physical bodies return to dust, our spirits will go on living. That is why my spirit yearns for my creator's energy the way a child yearns for a parent, or the lost yearn to be found, or the foreigner yearns for his home. I have the desire to know God better, the way he already knows me. I understand that for me to live a full life, I must nourish my spirit with the same fervor I nourish all other areas of my life. *Going forward with faith is no longer an option; it is a necessity.*

I fight for you
like a warrior with purpose
and nothing to lose.
I belong with you
and you belong with me.
I'll never be ashamed
to say I live because
you exist in me.

Reborn a warrior

Without you
I am a naked branch
without the hope of growing leaves.

Without you
I am a seed without the soil
needed to bear its fruit.

Without you
I am hopeless dust,
thrown into the wind.

My soul yearns for its creator.

How can a mortal ever describe infinity?
To describe it would be like
attempting to reach the end of an ocean
or find its beginning.
It would be like searching for stars
hazed by jealous clouds.
It would be like attempting
to understand fire and its wrath
beyond mythology and gods.
It would be like searching for silence in
    a storm
or walking on water without faith.
How can I expect a mortal to
    understand all of the universe's
    mysteries?
It's the knowledge that a mind like mine
    constantly seeks.

When I learned to see

If I had been born with material riches,
perhaps I would never have understood
abundant riches.

First I needed to let go
of what the flesh considers valuable
in order to understand life's true value.

Peace in the midst of the calamity.
Joy in the midst of the pain.
Faith in the midst of uncertainty.
Love in the midst of hate.

And that is when
I finally understood
what having riches in glory actually meant.

When I asked for abundance

I am a paradox.
Angels and demons
fight for my soul.

I hope the angels fight harder.

So many lost souls.
I only recognize them because
I've been lost too.

Familiarity

Faith is an everyday action.
I choose to believe.
I choose to hold on.
I choose to believe that one touch
of God's favor can change my life.

When I pray

8"

Maybe because
I want it so badly
it continues to flee from me.

Doubt

Something occurred to me after my last heartbreak; my naivete was completely gone, and my faith was tested. I'm not sure how many disappointments one heart can endure, but I do know there was a time when disappointment was all I knew. Sadly, I began to question if I was ever going to find the nurturing, trusting love my soul was seeking. What if in this lifetime I am only supposed to experience pain—the excruciating pain of unrequited love? What if I'll never see all my dreams come to pass? I picked myself up every time after the miserable spirit of doubt attacked my mind and heart. I courageously reminded myself that I must hold on to hope. After all, who am I without hope? Who am I without love?

At times, I allowed the worst doubts to consume me. The battlefield of the mind can encompass endless hours of thought. The constant wrestling of negative versus positive thoughts persists; ultimately, it affects our mental and emotional health. I have self-created migraines as a result. The idea of unbecoming is dreadful and can weigh any being down. Many times I questioned how to overpower the doubts that plagued me. In different circumstances, I have tried to analyze the effect of doubt on my spirit and the origin of that doubt.

One day as I typed the writing *w*'s—*what, where, who, why, when*—I received a clue on how humans create doubt. Every time we use any of these *w*'s, we can transform a sentence into a question, and the act of questioning opens the door for doubt. I applied that simple idea to my spiritual life. If I'm a woman who trusts the process and has faith in the path my creator designed for me, if I use the words *when, why, who, what, where,* I am then questioning my destiny. I unknowingly delay the outcome of the things I believe in and pray for. Every time I question the timing of *when* my dreams will come to pass, *when* I will get the career opportunity I've been waiting for, *when* I will get the healing my body needs, *when* I will meet the right partner, I am simply telling my creator, "I don't have enough faith because I keep questioning your timing." My heart does not intend to set me back, but the mind is powerful; it can create and destroy.

I made a decision to take charge and fight the doubt that has often dragged me down, that made me question all the wonderful things I envisioned for my life. Every morning I begin my day by deprogramming negative thoughts and replacing them with positive thoughts. I do so by meditation and prayer, and by reading and speaking positive affirmations that strengthen my faith and mind. I start my day with a grateful and open heart. It is my way of being proactive in welcoming and receiving the goodness and abundance of love, health, and prosperity already in store for me. I must speak as if I am an embodiment of all those things. I must admit some days the positivity comes more naturally than others, and some days life feels like a heavy task. Nonetheless, I'm taking life for what it is—*an evolution of growth. And it takes much courage to stay on course.*

The gift of the dreamer
is to have learned the courage
to overpower
the doubt that often crowds the mind.

To dream a bigger dream

I ran so far away
that the sun hid from me
and the moon couldn't find me.
Yet the land heard my heart's cry
and sought me out in the midst of my tempest.
My roots were screaming
for their seeds.

Lost and found

8"

What happens when trust is broken?

Lies, doubt, fear overpower the mind.
That leads to love being diminished.
That is damaging for the soul.
Our love is meant to expand
because real love is infinite.

Wretched is the person who first said
too good to be true.
Someone must have
stabbed his heart.
The bitterness spread
across the seas,
surviving centuries,
affecting all our lives.

Generational curses

8

There is a lesson in everything we live
    through
including every love.
I had to ask myself many times,
what did I seek in a relationship?
How did I want to feel?
When I began answering those questions,
I noticed I was piecing together all the
    men I had loved
into one perfect man.
The passion I felt with one,
the intellect of another,
or the childlike happiness I felt with
    others.
I kept comparing the new one
to how the old one made me feel,
never giving him a fair chance
unless he could immediately
do better than how the others made
    me feel.
I've robbed myself of much happiness
and honest love stories.

All because I feared that the new might
not reach the heights of the old

I am a collection of stories that I don't have the power to erase. That is why sometimes I feel more deeply than others, why at times I find it difficult to move forward. Sometimes I have the urge to escape. It is as if my freedom is hidden away in some corner of the world, and I must go on a whirlwind search for it. Anxiety wakes me up at night and shortens my breath. It's like a spirit that travels through rooms until it finds its prey. Sadly, on many nights I am its prey—I am tied to its leash, holding on to life, praying for air, rebuking its thoughts. I hate feeling helpless. The agonizing pressure I sometimes give myself. The knot in my chest I can't get rid of. Those nights I let my tears flow, and I let it be. My soul calls out for peace to take control and calmly run through my body like a river. If peace fails to rescue me, I succumb to the anxiety and call it madness.

My own unique madness

9"

Some people experience physical war,
but all I know
is the war within.

Selfishness

When I consider the power of decisions, I can't help but think of the lessons learned from each one—what they are, what the consequences have been, and what I eventually learned from them. My twenties were a roller coaster of emotions ruled by the heart and ideas ruled by the mind. At twenty-five, I found myself in love, with hopes of building a future with one particular man. We were inseparable—true best friends. We had a genuine connection, but his heart was troubled. Childhood traumas left marks that I lacked the power to erase. Nonetheless, I embarked on a love story with him. A year and half into our relationship, I dreamed I was pregnant and when I had the baby, my boyfriend wasn't as present as I expected. The dream fast-forwarded to the baby as a toddler. The child had a mix of my eyes and his face shape, one that was prominent in his family. It was as if I saw an alternate destiny with him, one filled with uncertainty. I awoke and looked at him still asleep, wondering if the unhappiness I foresaw in my dream would ever become a reality.

I've heard some women say they knew exactly the moment they became pregnant. Caribbean Latin culture is vivid and full of superstition. Single women never let anyone sweep close to their feet because that could bring them bad luck finding a husband. I prided myself on not believing in folklore and superstition, but in my blood runs a lineage of women with wonderful spiritual gifts and abilities. Foreshadowing dreams were among those gifts. Months after the pregnancy dream, a chaotic period in every part of my life began. I developed a contagious skin condition that shook me to my core. I feared that after my skin healed, I would be scarred forever. My boyfriend was extremely supportive and was not afraid to touch me. He helped me believe my skin would heal and I'd be back to my normal self in no time. Then, to make things worse, my finances hit a low point, and I had to move out of the home I loved into an apartment I wasn't fond of. I found myself reevaluating my life. I had chosen an unstable, artistic career that depended a lot on my physical attributes, and I became full of fear and regrets. To add to the pressure, my period was late. I was on the pill, and I had always been pretty regular. Since I was under so much emotional and physical stress, I assumed my body was reacting to my circumstances. But my dream from months before popped into my mind, and I became nervous. It couldn't be. I drove to the nearest drugstore to buy a pregnancy test, and at home, just like in a bad movie, the positive line appeared. In that moment the fear that already possessed me multiplied, and I had to face my reality.

I immediately made an appointment at a local women's clinic. I still had a sliver of hope that the test was wrong. I thought through all the possible scenarios as the day went on—to have a baby or not. My boyfriend was out of town, and when I told him the news he accepted it and left the choice up to me. At the clinic, the doctor performed an ultrasound; he confirmed my pregnancy, and we learned I was exactly four weeks pregnant. My due date was 11-11-11, a lucky date for so many others. Since the pregnancy was at such an early stage, I was given the option of taking an abortion pill. I was told there would be a lot of pain involving extremely sharp cramps, and I couldn't be alone for the first twenty-four hours. I had a decision to make.

9

I was tormented. My life was a mess, and I wasn't ready to care for a child. Because of my religious upbringing, I was filled with shame even to think about an abortion. I didn't want to disappoint my parents. I also didn't want to be another unwed mother, like my sister before me. When she became pregnant with my nephew, my father didn't speak to her for months, and her life was filled with chaos. I weighed my options, and within days, I chose to terminate the pregnancy. I figured the faster I did it the less attached I'd become to the idea of a life growing inside me. I wasn't far along enough to experience any pregnancy symptoms like nausea, morning sickness, or cravings. My body didn't change in those few weeks either. On the outside everything seemed the same—the only proof I had was that tiny dot on the ultrasound. It was the most meaningful dot. A dot that could change my life forever. Although change is inevitable, I wasn't ready for more of it then. At five weeks, I ended the pregnancy, and that time in my life became just another secret locked away in a vault with the rest of them. But you see, the thing about secrets is that no matter how well you hide them, they never go away. They exist in your mind, and they echo in your heart.

I understand there are people who will judge me, and I confess I have also judged myself. But I do know there are also those who will understand me and relate to the confusion and struggle I experienced during that period. There were many times I came close to telling my mother, especially since I always feel as if she can see right through me. But sadly, I was never brave enough. It's interesting that we fear tarnishing someone else's opinion of us, yet we are forced to face our own opinion of ourselves on a daily basis. Two years after I made that difficult decision, my relationship fell apart in a hurtful way. A part of me was thankful I didn't go through with the pregnancy. The pain of how we separated surely could have traumatized the child and perhaps even created identity issues as the years went by. After all, we are products of our environments, and the first five years of a child's life can potentially shape the rest of it. Regardless, after much self-reflection, I understood my decision was based on pure selfishness, and love isn't meant to be selfish. I never intended to be that way, but I accept it as one of the most selfish decisions I ever made. I only thought of *me* and how the pregnancy could negatively impact my life at the time. Not once did I think of the blessing it could have been for me or the father. Now that I understand what unconditional love is, I believe my pregnancy was a test on many levels. Some might think I failed the test, but when I finally understood unconditional love, I learned that it starts with ourselves. I learned to love, forgive, and accept myself. After all, we aren't born with the answers to all the questions life brings us. We are also not born with perfect knowledge of what love is. We learn about the types of love through the journey of life. It took loss and suffering for me to learn about my own selfishness and my capacity to learn selflessness. I have learned that unconditional love involves sacrifice and giving without expecting a return. As I continue to grow and learn, I can see that I am indeed passing the test because I am continuously striving to be a better version of myself.

Since 2011, every time I see 11-11 on a time stamp or calendar, I think of how old my child would be. Sometimes his cute little face from the foreshadowing dream pops up. I no longer shed tears—as with all of my other losses, I have learned to accept the destiny I chose, the decisions I made then and make today. I can't continue to live in the past if I intend to live a full life. I have learned to look brightly toward the future, and I believe I can still have the life I've always dreamed of. My past is part of me, but I refuse to allow it to define me. *I am a woman with many layers. I am proud of all those layers because they are what makes me genuinely me.*

I struggle
with the responsibility
of knowing *how to love.*

There are days
when I am an overflowing fountain
of compassion and empathy.

Then there are days
when I am a dry well
hiding from my own shadow.

I am far from perfect.

9"

The search for perfection has ruined
   my days.
Perfection doesn't exist,
everyone chooses to say.
Then why must I not make any
   mistakes?
What makes me different from
   anyone else?

The pressures we trigger on those whom
we say we love

Break down,
shatter into pieces.
Then build yourself back up
and shout out to the world.
I did it for myself
I did it for you.
To prove that masterpieces
aren't always valued
when the fickle public first sees them.

They'll call me arrogant when they
should've called me brave.

There's a loneliness knocking down
my door this evening.
It wants to creep in
like daybreak
and make my heart its home.

I refuse to let it in.

On a night like this
all I'm missing
are feelings.

When I'm cold

I swore to forget
your face.
Yet I see you everywhere.
I spar with our memories,
and still—
the feeling of you
doesn't leave me.

You still haunt me.

10"

The problem between us:
there is too much touch
and not enough intimacy.

Intimacy

In my life, the most memorable moments have been when I experienced true intimacy. Sadly, it took me many years to understand how meaningful and unforgettable those moments are. Two people can connect profoundly when they share stories that impacted their lives and made them who they are. Stories of joyous or broken childhoods. Stories of a first kiss or a first heartbreak. The anecdotes behind pivotal successes and failures. We develop intimacy with another human being the moment we release the fear of judgment and allow space for vulnerability. Intimacy becomes a silent pact between two kindred souls. Suddenly, two strangers begin to see into each other. They become empathetic toward each other. They learn about the fragility of trust.

Sometimes I observe people and wonder how I am like them. What common experiences do we share? Have we hurt or loved the same? Do we have similar dreams or passions? Have you ever fallen in love with someone's mind without ever touching them? I have. Lay on the same bed, yet never kissed. Looked deep into their eyes, without speaking. Developed a deep connection and felt comfort with certain individuals whom I never saw again. I've also done the opposite. Been physically intimate with someone without knowing his aspirations. Without knowing his full name. Lived the moment of skin on skin with animalistic instincts instead of real connection, which eventually made me feel empty and ashamed. All because I've gone against my true nature. I was created to connect with other humans and form true intimacy.

On a rainy day, I had a chance encounter with a past lover. We were at the same gathering, and for the first time in years, we had a few minutes alone. We left the building together. He asked the question that has a hundred answers, "How are you?" I smiled while my heartbeat regained normal speed. Why answer what he was able to read with one look? After all, he was one of the few people with the power to look into my eyes and see directly into my soul. Then, he held me the way only he knows. I felt sincerity through his embrace. It was as if our souls had expressed the same affection in every lifetime, and the energy between us spoke without words. As he continued to hold me, the hectic street noise of the mid-city traffic became silent. In those moments, all I could hear was my heartbeat recognizing his. He tilted his head back and looked at me. His eyes looked directly into mine, and he smiled. Over a decade after our affair, we stood silent, knowing we had something that time hadn't changed. Time had only added the soft lines around his eyes and the gray in his hair and in mine. His lips still had a magnetic attraction to my skin; he planted a kiss on my cheek and told me he loved me. I still loved him as well, and I'm convinced I will never stop loving him. Saying goodbye to someone you love is always heartbreaking, and lord knows I wish we could have run away and left behind all the responsibilities of the lives we built without each other—*but how selfish would that be?* The sky drizzled its tears onto us as we pulled away and said goodbye. Moments later he called my name. When I turned, I saw his mischievous smile, and I called out his. In that split second, I was reminded of the intimacy we had formed so long ago. I believe that intimacy will always connect us regardless of the lost years and separate destinies. I couldn't help but be emotional throughout the rest of that day because with him, it seems there is never enough closure; in my life he will remain unforgettable.

I yearn for that type of intimacy again. The feeling of knowing someone well enough and forming such a strong connection that it can survive lifetimes. A connection of that magnitude feeds my soul. It gives me hope and a sense of belonging. I also feel that being able to understand that level of intimacy has given me another understanding of life. I am able to take a peek at someone else's heart, and I allow them to take a look into mine. Intimacy is as sexy as it is tender. It is as passionate as it is passive. *It's a mutual admiration.*

Eighteen Inches

It is far beyond touch.
It is far beyond a butterfly spreading its wings.
It is far beyond revealing skin.
It is far beyond body language
and chemistry between two bodies.

It is the way you discreetly move my hair
away from my face.
It is the way you surprise my foot
under a table.
It is the way you manage
to dip my bread in olive oil
before it reaches my mouth.

It is the way I whisper
sweet nothings in your ear.
It is the way your eyes
have the power
to burn a smile into my soul
from across a room.

It is something you and I possess,
a certain dialect,
a certain understanding free of judgment.
It is the ability to carry each other
in the darkest of days,
in the coldest winters,
in the shortest summers.

You and I form true intimacy.

You and I
could have set roots.
We could have planted
a garden.

But sadly, we didn't.

Colliding with your fragments
is not enough.
I have the urge
to know you whole,
your nature
and your lore.
The old soul
bathing in your eyes.
The hidden gems
that make you smile.
Tapping your surface
is not enough.

My desire is to know you whole.

I miss loving someone
so strongly that my breathing fails me.
I miss those moments
silent but palpable.
I miss when I'm known well enough
to have my mind read.
I miss living awake
because these days I only live asleep
dreaming of the beyond,
escaping the routine.
I miss those kisses full of madness
when you know that your lover's lips
are more yours than his.
I miss those days when I touched the sky,
days that are now recorded
in every joint of my anatomy.
How to erase experience?
How to erase the knowledge
of something so unique and special?
How to erase you from me?
When everything you are is mixed
            with mine.

How does one erase experience?

It's a scary thing when I,
a woman of many words,
begin to lack the words
to express how I feel.
You hold my words hostage
and leave me speechless.

That is what you do to me.

Today, I do not sweat.
Instead, I shiver.
The sun says
it's a different day.
The rain says
it's a different climate.
Yet my body says
it's the same illness.

I still miss you.

When I see you
I have a sudden urge
to caress your face,
to gently take my fingers
and wipe away the invisible tears of your
pain.
To press my chest against yours,
and to feel your heartbeat speeding
at the moment we touch.
All I want is to bring my lips close to yours
and bring comfort to your soul.
When I see you
my strongest urge
is to feel you,
to love you,
and to hold you
as I did before.

Wanting what no longer is mine

Thank you,
for all the words that you gave me.

And yes,
I still feel a gravity pull
when I happen to see you.

11"

*Humans take everything
and corrupt it.*

Sex

Sex does not define love, and love should not define sex. Is it a need, the way humans have made it out to be? Or is it simply pleasure? An amazing pleasure. I had an orgasm while I slept one afternoon. It was smack in the middle of the day. I was on the verge of depression. Every planet in my life was in retrograde that month. I felt as if everything was going wrong. I fell asleep crying, and suddenly my sleep turned into a provocative dream in which I ran into a past lover whom I had a fiery sexual attraction to. In the dream, we both tried to fight the sexual tension since we were with others. The crowd around us could feel our tension, and I could tell it made them nervous—that turned us on even more. The intensity between us escalated; it kept escalating. My breathing synced with his, quick and short and fast until we both took one large breath, and as we exhaled, we stripped off each other's clothes. We began to have sex—passionate and voyeuristic sex. Everyone was watching. Since I was asleep and in a relaxed state, I quickly elevated to an orgasm. If only falling asleep during an afternoon were always that pleasurable. How was I able to orgasm so intensely in a dream when in the flesh it seems like such a task? How can the love I have for another human being not be enough to experience any level of climax, especially of that magnitude? It hurt to know the truth. It's as if when men created sex, they learned how to orgasm and forgot about women.

The first time I had sex, I experienced an orgasm. I quickly thought sex was everything it was talked up to be, true ecstasy. I was nineteen, and the young man who took my virginity knew enough to take his time to please me. Sex isn't a selfish, one-minute thing; it is a process, one that is meant to be enjoyed by both people.

My first lover taught me the importance of being relaxed during sex and allowing my mind to be free without inhibitions. Still, six months later I broke up with him. Although I felt madly loved by him, he and I were polar opposites. He had few life ambitions, and I had too many. He had strong abandonment issues, and I didn't love him enough to spend my life trying to fix him. Nonetheless, he taught me about sex and damaged me at the same time. The worst experience is to know sexual satisfaction and then not receive it again for a long time. At times I asked myself if something was wrong with me. Is my body rejecting the man I love? Why can't I orgasm while having sex?

Our society has done an awful thing—it has conditioned people to continuously blame themselves for everything that goes wrong in their lives, and sex is one of them. First, I had to understand that I wasn't alone. Most women have questioned their sexuality, had sexual questions, or needed to find their own sexual expression. All of the questions I had on sex were completely normal—the problem was, who would answer them? I had to remove the sexual stigma from my conservative upbringing. I also had to heal from the sexual traumas I had experienced. I decided that I was a woman who wanted to experience the same pleasures most men do. Sex didn't have to be perverse, the way certain groups make it out to be. I decided that the quality of my sex life was a personal choice. That was the conversation I began to have with myself. I had to discover what I liked and how to achieve it. After all, everyone's body operates differently, and I had to find my own sexual expression. I realized it was up to me and only me to add the brilliant colors of good sex to my life. *All the things I have always desired outside of love; after all, it's human nature.*

The torment of a flashback
disrupting my peace.
Now, how do I remove
the image of his vitality
thrusting into me?
And what of his endurance
as he leaves his mark on me?
Or what of the memory of his sweat
meeting my skin?
And what of his haunting eyes
piercing my soul?
The sweet,
sweet torment
of reliving him once more.

Torment me again.

Everyone has a vice.
I don't know which is worse—
to be physically
or mentally
addicted to someone?

Both have brought me suffering.

I want to tell you about
how you disrupt my sleep.
I want to tell you about the power
you have over me.
I want to tell you about your name
and how, when it comes up,
it brings chills to me.
Maybe I'm weak or
maybe thoughts of you
are taking full control of me.
I've lost my grip,
now I'm naked
and feel powerless.
All while I convince you
that what you and I have
is only pure lust.

Things I never told him

I can't seem to rip your scent
off my bones.
It wasn't oud,
nor sage, nor wood.
Was I a fool?
Loved too boldly but not enough.
Why did I choose to love you the way a
mortal loves?

When you and I were stars

12"

To live a truthful life, one must learn to be assertive.

Fulfillment

To feel at peace, to be content and without the longing for something missing. That is how I define personal fulfillment. I'd be lying if I said all my dreams have come to fruition. I don't think I'll ever stop dreaming as long as I'm alive. Dreams are very much tied to my hopes for the future, and the same hopes are tied to my happiness. What I have learned is that to feel fulfilled, one doesn't necessarily have to achieve all those dreams yet, or ever, but one must be content during the process. Sometimes I think of Moses, and I wonder how he felt to have never set foot in the Promised Land. Did he ever feel unfulfilled because of that? Or was he able to pass away peacefully, knowing that he was able to fulfill his purpose of helping his people?

There are many areas of my life in which I strive for more success, and many times I come up short. Most of my life I've had to learn as I go, without a manual or mentor. I still have much more learning to do, and I'm excited to see what the future will bring. I admit that while trying to navigate through life, I have compared myself to other women. I'm not ashamed to admit it. I have compared myself to women I personally know, and some whom I admire from afar. Sometimes other people's lives appear to be more fascinating or more complete than mine. I have felt curious to know about things that other women do—what it would be like to visit certain countries, speak other languages, give back more, have children and a husband, have another career or simply another lifestyle. Many of the women I compare myself to have inspired me, but I also wonder if they are truly happy and if they indeed feel fulfilled, because I know too well that appearances can be deceiving.

At times I think back on my earlier life and reflect on my decisions. One that haunts more than others was the decision to leave my hometown. I was very young and felt my destiny was elsewhere, but it meant parting from my family and my oldest nephew. Some might think, "Well, he wasn't your child." But he is the closest thing to a son I've ever experienced. He is the light of my life, even when his quietness worries me. One of his smiles can make my day perfect. I genuinely have every one of his smiles engraved in my mind. How he was at one year old, at three, at five, at seven, as a teen. All this love I have felt for him will never make up for the fact that I left, that perhaps he grew up feeling his *titi* chose bigger dreams than being by his side at all times. I blame myself for the pain he has lived, as if my love and presence could have protected him from the stress of his parents' constant fighting, the pain of his father's unexpected passing, or from the anxiety that made him grow up faster than he should have. I wonder if I would feel more fulfilled if I had stayed physically closer to him, for I am convinced his soul and mine are beautifully connected. But then I think, if I had stayed, how fulfilled as a woman would I be? Would I have ever quenched my desires for more? Back then, I told myself I was leaving to fulfill my career dreams so I could give him the things I lacked growing up, so he could feel proud of me. I'm not sure how well I have succeeded, except that I feel peace in knowing we have the same connection we've had since I first held him in my arms.

Everyone has a different definition of fulfillment. It's quite personal, and it exists within the walls of our own minds. Our thoughts create the standards for our own fulfillment. In moments of solitude, I listen to my crowded thoughts and allow gratitude and acceptance to sink in. I accept that there are things I cannot change, and I must focus on what I can change. Many nights when sleep evades me, I ask myself, "Do you feel fulfilled?" Many days I do. I feel content where I am in life and where life is taking me. Then on the days that I don't feel that way, I ask myself, "What should I change? What areas need improvement?" I think the negative emotions I have felt are largely influenced by outside sources and by my own personal expectations. The twenty-year-old me expected the future me to have it all. Anyway, what is *all*? The universe certainly laughs at our expectations because life can't be planned. It's meant to be lived. My life today is the complete opposite of what I planned sitting in my pink-and-white room in Miami, but I believe it's exactly the way it was meant to be. Either I choose to believe that everything happens for a reason and works out for a greater good, or I take a bitter approach to life's disappointments. That's an approach I refuse to take—why not be content and choose gratitude? When I choose gratitude, I see the abundance of favor I've been given. I realize that it is in my nature to strive for new heights, but I understand that I have the power to be fulfilled and loved at any stage in my life.

I am convinced
no golden age lasts.
At some point
the earth must shake
under our feet
as a reminder that invisibility
only belongs to God.

Reminders

Children never know the value of a coin
until they learn that sweat and work
earned that coin.

Young people never find wisdom
until experience and pain
mature them by force.

Adults never understand living in the
        present
until they are closer
to breathing their last breath.

I continue learning.

Humans yearn to belong
and to be loved.
They become parents,
they become lovers,
they establish friendships,
simply to fulfill the quiet need to love,
to be loved,
and to connect.

Human connections

My brokenness
became
my breakthroughs.

Painful realization

Commitment?

I like the idea of it.
It's comforting for me to know
I've always had my own back,
and someone else made the choice
to have my back too.

13"

In the midst of the chaos,
focus on the things
that bring you joy.

Happiness

There was a time when I believed happiness was fleeting; then I learned that happiness is a choice. To be happy is a constant decision I make every day regardless of how things in my life are going. It's a gratitude that must come from within—gratitude for everything, including things we often take for granted. My attitude toward happiness changed when I was able to focus on what I had rather than what I lacked. I disrupted my destination mentality and replaced it with a gratitude mentality. After all, to have needs and to want are two very different things.

I used to think when I accomplished certain goals or attained a certain amount of success I would be overwhelmed by happiness. Ultimately, I understood how wrong that was because my happiest moments were always those I spent with my family and loved ones. The smiles of discovery from my nieces and nephews. The uncontrollable laughter with friends. The beautiful sunsets that remind me how small I am in the larger universe of things. The embrace of a loved one on a rainy day. It wasn't that I didn't appreciate the little things; the problem was that I was constantly waiting for something bigger to arrive and was never satisfied with living the present itself.

I was born in the Dominican Republic, which has a large share of poverty. But when tourists describe my people, they express surprise at the abundance of contagious happiness. In my adult life, I have been fortunate to have visited other beautiful destinations around the world. Throughout my travels I have always been amazed to witness the amount of happiness and joy exerted by citizens of forgotten, poverty-stricken countries. Their smiles radiate the energy of gratitude for things many of us take for granted. Something as simple as the sun and rain needed for crops or clean water to drink. These people might never know the world outside their village, yet they radiate joy. My birth country is on an island of stunning beaches, yet many have never seen the ocean because they can't pay for bus fare. Then there are the women who walk for hours to fetch clean water for their families and are never too tired to wave and smile at a stranger passing by. In contrast, I've taken for granted countless warm baths and find it shocking when a stranger smiles at me. Then there are the men who feel strong satisfaction when they find materials to build a shack for their families. I have often closed my eyes at night without giving thanks for the home I have. These realizations have stirred my heart, and I've asked myself if I must witness what others lack in order to understand how blessed I am. Is ignorance truly bliss? Can having less knowledge of the world secure more happiness? If I had less compared to others, would I be more grateful? I realize I don't have any excuses not to be happy. I am blessed in many areas. All my needs are met, and I am blessed to have more than most. I also understand that happiness is much like beauty—it's all in perspective. I can't teach anyone outside of myself to be happy. It doesn't matter how hard I try or how available I am. Happiness is not forced; it is a personal decision. Everyone must make that choice for him or herself. To be happy is perhaps the single most important choice I have made and continue to make. I've slowed down and taken the time to appreciate the beauty around me. I admire the sunsets with different eyes than before, and I receive the smiles of strangers as I never did before. *Gratitude causes my heart to smile, and happiness blooms from all the gratitude.*

Our love is sprinkled across all the matter
we call suns and stars.
Lighting fires
of love and passion
much like you and I.

The universe has a place for stories like ours.

If we reap
what we sow,
then those who love
deserve to be loved.

I know what I deserve.

He'll never get bored with her.
The moment he thinks
he has her figured out
is the moment
she'll introduce him
to the other seven women
who exist in her.

I am her.

I want to tangle my legs
around you and be still.
Soak in your presence
while we hear the birds shriek,
envious of our affection.

So happy even the birds envy us

14"

You want it now,
when there is no now.
There is only always.

Patience

If I were asked what is the one lesson I was meant to learn in this lifetime, I would most likely answer *have patience*. When I was a little girl, I remember throwing tantrums when I lost something and couldn't find it after a quick search. The tantrums decreased as I got older, especially since after each one, my mother would remind me of a biblical verse on patience being a virtue. It didn't matter how much a man worried; he still couldn't add a cubit to his stature. So right before the frustration and tantrum kicked in, I'd try to breathe and tell myself to calm down and practice patience. Whatever I was looking for would eventually turn up! Yet even after the tantrums were gone, I became an expert at leaping to conclusions. I have been the girl who blew up her boyfriend's phone when she didn't receive a speedy response. One time I felt pretty stupid because the reason he didn't call was that he was simply taking a nap. Unfortunately, my impatient behavior demanded that things go my way and on my time schedule. What a battle. But how could I reduce my impulsivity and learn to be patient?

I wish I could say that I have it all figured it out, but I don't. Patience is still a virtue I haven't fully mastered. Yet knowing that it's an area where I'm weak, patience remains in the back of my mind. It's as if I'm constantly monitoring myself and my reactions. I hear my mother's voice, and I breathe a little more slowly as a truth sinks in—*find the calm in the storm*. I take my time, I don't rush, I stay still, and I find my patience. The only way I can learn to master my weaknesses is by practice. I'm always impressed by people who can write calligraphy because there is so much patience involved in that art. It's a talent that is learned over time and mastered by practice. What the calligrapher innately possesses is a patient spirit. I believe that our personality traits are, in reality, spirits residing within us—spirits that flow in and out depending on what doors we leave open. When people knock at my door, I have the choice to either let them in or leave them outside. I realize that spiritually we have the power to decide which spirits can create a home within us because we are creators in our own right. Now when I meditate and practice being still, I welcome the spirit of patience. *I allow it to work within me so it will cause change, challenge me, and make me better.*

Valor, oh valor,
where did my valor come from?
From the trance of loving you—
or the lesson in losing you?

When I feel I've lost my grip
and my arms are tired from holding on,
when I feel I'm drowning
in a dark ocean,
there is a light that suddenly rescues me
and bursts in like a sunbreak.

That light is you.

To rise above my limitations,
to see beyond the horizon,
to learn that silence is part of listening,
to practice the art of stillness,
all those have led me to finding virtues.

15"

And what do I constantly want?
Love and Adventure.
I want a love that takes me on the best
adventure of my life.

Adventure

It all happened one summer—at a time when women everywhere felt more united. It was when I felt the strongest, but also the most detached I had ever been. I wasn't completely numb yet, but I was on the verge. I am a woman of many words, commanded by so much emotion, but at that time, I was running low on my passion for life. I embarked on a trip to renew my zest for life; it eventually taught me one of the most valuable lessons I've learned about love and friendship.

My adventure began in Paris, and it immediately involved a week of making new acquaintances and a series of serendipitous events. I attended the opening of an exhibition and heard the tagline being thrown around as part of a campaign by a legendary fashion house. It said, "And you? What would you do for love?" I searched for my answer within, but like most truths, the answer actually popped up without much effort. My heart silently shouted, "I'd travel the world to find that love!" I looked around at the posh guests, curious about how they would answer the question. Were they also on a quest, as I was, or were they satisfied with their lives in the present?

The next day I went to dinner with a friend who has always shown affection toward me, but I have never responded the way he deserves. He drank whiskey, and I drank a dry white wine. In his heavy French accent, but with a soft-toned voice, he looked at me with piercing blue eyes and said, "I am simply here to be a witness to your happiness." I looked at him dumbfounded, because I had nothing to give him. For the first time in a long time, I couldn't speak. It was as if I was empty. My immediate reaction was to take a swig of my wine. I looked up at him through my false lashes, wondering if he understood that I didn't feel the same. He dreamed of being with me, but I was on another quest. I wasn't sure exactly what I was searching for, but I believed that when I found it, my heart would beat and my soul would jump out to grab it.

Days later, I was on a plane to Croatia with a group of friends. It was a last-minute trip, one I decided to take the day before at a Parisian amusement park between a carousel ride and a glass of cheap red wine. Without thinking twice, I had booked a flight to Croatia right there and then, believing it was destiny since there was only one seat left on the same flight my friends had already booked. Would I have a summer love, or would nothing romantic occur? Every other day I received a message from my mother asking if I had met someone *interesting*. As if my fulfillment as a woman or my joy during that summer depended solely on having a man enter my life.

The members of our group couldn't have been any more different, but I liked that. Our first discovery was that Croatian wine was very good, and boy, did we have plenty. We spent long days dipping in the Adriatic Sea, long dinners talking about everything under the moon, and long afternoons discovering salty bays of stunning aquamarine water. With every discovery I made about each one of my friends, I made one about myself. I bonded with them on a deeper level than would ever have happened at home, and for that I was grateful. Many stories later, our trip came to an end, and I was ready to meet another group of friends in Ibiza.

It wasn't the first time I had visited the island, but I was excited to explore another side of it with different people. I quickly discovered everything about that magical island. Many myths surround its legendary history, and there was a dark side to many of them. Some days were hazy, but I dared to push myself to feel again.

One afternoon I left my room and headed toward the main dining table of the villa where breakfast and lunch were always served. I walked past a new face, a man with a glowing Mediterranean tan; his tall frame occupied the entire sofa. It was obvious it had been a long night for him. Lunch was served, and surprisingly, he found the energy to join us. His smile was bright and contagious, and it overpowered the hangover he was probably experiencing. I quickly became enchanted. Thirty minutes into lunch, I knew too little but enough about him. He was married, but he made it seem to be an unhappy union. I wondered how a man so full of life could end up trapped in an unsuccessful marriage. This dashing man had married into incredible wealth, and I thought that it would be difficult for him to part with the private jets, yachts, different homes around the world, access, power. But what about love? I didn't know him enough to know the answer to that question, but I was curious to know more.

I would be lying if I said my attraction to him was purely physical. He was also bright and well rounded. I wanted to pick his brain about everything he knew. The way he conversed with others was genuine. I looked away many times when he looked at me. I blushed and hid my smile. I spent days in his company, but I escaped from a quiet temptation. Regardless of his unhappy marriage, he seemed to be faithful, and I admired that. His last night on the island arrived. He would soon jet off to meet his wife and child at some exotic location where one of her yachts was anchored. Four of us sat at a small, round table overlooking the pool. We discussed the world we lived in, our romances, and failed relationships. For the first time, I looked at him without intimidation and asked how he had proposed to his wife. He responded: "It was at a pizza drive-thru—I was starving, and she wouldn't shut up about how she needed commitment. So I said, 'OK, you can move in,' and that turned into a proposal. Two months later, we were married." I was shocked; it was unromantic and disappointing, but at least he was honest. A half hour later, we joined the rest of the group. The techno music playing throughout the house all sounded the same in my head, but I was at ease and felt free. His energetic smile caught my eye once more, and I understood that for his love of wealth, he had sacrificed another kind of love. Although I couldn't bear the idea of choosing money over love, I tried to let go of judging him. I smiled with him because I saw that he found his freedom on nights like this.

There were no wasted days that summer. Ibiza quickly became Italy, where I had embarked on a road trip with one of my best friends. We explored the Italian Riviera and discovered the beauty of Cinque Terre. There was a certain magic to Ibiza—a Peter Pan type of magic—but in Cinque Terre there was an old-world atmosphere. During our first night in one of the tiny villages that make up the national park, we had dinner at a small restaurant that quickly became our restaurant of choice during our stay. It had the best pasta my friend and I have ever had! We met a family celebrating their child's high school graduation and had drinks with them at the village cantina. They slurred their words from too much tequila, but one thing was obvious—those parents loved their children and wanted the best for them. The way the woman looked at her daughter reminded me a lot of how my mother looks at me. Every mother has dreams for her child, the blood of her blood. I saw that she wanted her daughter to have many experiences, to perhaps make different choices than she had because now the rules were different.

The next day we rented a tiny wooden boat for a few hours. We wanted to explore the other villages. We saw the beauty of the area, heard its history, dove into its waters, and swam through its caves. I began to fall in love. I was reminded that sometimes the simpler life is the happiest one. There we were on a small wooden boat discovering beautiful waters, toasting under the sun, and having the time of our lives. We were completely oblivious to all the fancy environments we'd experienced earlier on the trip. I looked at my friend of over sixteen years, and I told her that there was no one else I would rather be with at that moment. Such a special moment with such a real friend. Others might have wished to be there with a romantic partner because it was a romantic place, but I felt as if life was teaching me to appreciate another face of love.

In religion and mythology, the deities have different names dependent on their personal qualities. Love is no different. Love has many attributes and, therefore, many faces, but it is up to us to be receptive to those different faces of love. If I had fallen in romantic love that summer, perhaps I wouldn't have been able to dwell in the beauty of my friendship. I would've spent my time focusing on only one face of love, when love has many. Instead, I chose freedom to live and not be confined by what was expected of me. When my mother asked me again if I had met anyone interesting, I replied: "Yes, Mami, I have. I've met many interesting people. I now have more friends and experiences than I had yesterday."

Toward the end of our Italian adventure, I had an epiphany. I understood that I would never know if the opportunities I encounter are right or wrong when they appear—the objective is to learn to trust my soul path. I can find reasons for my failures and victories, but the point is to live and find what's genuine for me. Now I understand that the reason I didn't get everything I wanted was because I didn't appreciate the smaller, beautiful moments. I had to learn to accept that life is not about what we didn't get. It is always about wisdom gained and how we return it to the world—that is how we can learn to live.

I've had friends, romances, and careers, and I chose to love them in return. I've gained experiences, gifts, pleasures, joys, and pains, and I appreciated them in return. The true purpose of all of it was to learn about my connection to the divine. It is knowledge that exists beyond technology, status, or philosophy, and it is not bought with currency or exchanged with favors. It is achieved through gratitude and a connection with the living world and our creator. My heart was right when it told me I should travel the world for love. The mistake I made was believing the quest was for romantic love; instead, I found many of its other faces and was lucky enough to have known them in my life. *We all need reminders of what we'd do for love.*

15 "

I don't understand people
who are OK
with just being alive.

There's an entire life to live.

Isn't it ironic
that we fly in planes so freely,
yet how many of us
will ever learn to fly?

15″

People have a need to kiss.
Maybe it's an oral fixation.
As infants we sucked milk
from our mothers' breasts
or from bottles
without knowing that it would create
the need for kisses.
A certain affection
that makes people crave
and do absolutely ingenious things.
And so I ask myself,
how far would I go for that oral fixation?

Her cigarette burned him.
Like a disguised masochist,
he wanted more of it.
Simply because
that would be the closest
to his skin
she'll ever be.

People watching

When he kissed her
she placed her hands
on his chest.
And through his heartbeat,
she learned what it was like to feel again.

Teach me how to feel.

I think of everyone
I was meant to meet.
Who drove me
to meeting and losing you.
They are all gone.
Yet they served their purpose
because here I am
still inspired by you.

Everyone plays a part in the stage of life.

16"

Understand you were created from light.
Therefore, you radiate light.
Don't be afraid to shine.

Identity

Who am I? It's a question I have often asked myself. I found the answer through constant self-reflection, but I often struggle with the difference between who the world tells me I am and who I was created to be. The world has often been wrong when it has tried to define me because material belongings and labels will never define me. My circle of friends, family, or my exterior appearance do not define me either. Still, many times I have allowed my value as a person to be calculated by the standards of the outside world. I've been fooled into thinking that accolades, recognition, power, and flattery can provide anything more than a temporary feeling of satisfaction. It seems that these are the only things the world is drawn to, which, sadly, leaves most people empty. After all, we live in a spiritually bankrupt society—one that values what you have over who you are. How do I navigate through this world yet not belong to it? How do I reject being defined by the enormous array of images we are constantly bombarded with by the media? How do I feel confident in who I am, stay strong, and not easily be shaken or broken?

I have always found it amazing that people place such high importance on material things—when we pass, we can't take any of it with us. People think it is so important to be admired by strangers, yet when we pass, those people who said they loved us are quick to forget us. The world is fickle. People carry on such a relentless search for the next new thing because they lack a true identity. Many times I have succumbed to those feelings of insatiability, but to prove what? Every day the sun rises, the sun sets, the moon commands the tides; there is nothing on this Earth that I can humanly do that will ever be the equivalent of those miracles.

I find it hard to define myself by labels when they change so constantly. Today I am someone's daughter, but the day my parents pass on, who will I be? Today I am a writer, but if I stop writing, who will I be? Today I might be someone's wife, yet if we separate, who will I be then? If I choose not to be defined by my accomplishments, then why should I allow myself to be defined by the ever-changing crowd of people around me? There are responsibilities attached to labels. Why not define myself by the only thing that I know doesn't change: *the creator's love.* I consider myself an extension of the creator's energy, and his love. I believe we are all part of that same extension—it is part of our spiritual DNA. Consequently, if we strive for love at all times and in all roles, who we are will not change. I have chosen to live with the understanding that being love means some sacrifices, but it also has countless wonderful attributes. I choose to be defined by love's attributes, and that will give me a firm identity based on truth— *my personal truth.*

It took some time,
but now I can say
that I am all mine.

Accept yourself
before seeking belonging.

When I looked at him pacing around the
    room,
I saw in him a childish quality and a need
    to be held
similar to the men I loved before him.
I realized that my attraction to these men
    wasn't only physical,
it stemmed from my desire to help them,
to take them in my arms and make them
    whole,
make them feel loved.
In that moment I understood something
    had to change.
My desire to give love superseded
everything else I thought was magical in
    romance.
Giving love wasn't an option,
it was a necessity.

I am always torn among three women.
The woman I used to be,
the woman I am,
and the woman I hope to be.

Still, they all have flaws.

If you could unlearn
everything you've been taught
and relearn
through the pathway of your soul,
who would you be?

The soul remembers.

17"

People feel empty because they search for purpose in all the wrong places.

Purpose

We are all born with a purpose. No one's purpose is more important than another's. Some people's guiding principles might simply be more visible than others'. Every organ in the human body has a purpose—a contribution that makes the body run smoothly as it was designed. We were taught this fact, we believe it, but is it visible to the human eye? Do we see our arteries actually pumping our blood? Do we see our liver detoxing our body? Do we see our lungs pumping oxygen? No, but we are certain that every organ, every detail of the human body, was meticulously created with an important purpose that makes us function. If our bodies were designed to be temples of our souls, why do some people think their life on Earth has no purpose?

I cannot remember the first time I questioned what my purpose on Earth was, but I do remember the pivotal moment when I stumbled across it. I was an inquisitive child. I had many questions and was always seeking out answers. Inquisitive or not, most children naturally have questions because they are making their first discoveries of the world. They want to know how babies are made and what those little dots that brighten the night sky are; they want to pet animals without realizing they'll bite. They are drawn to playing with toys regardless of their culture. They pretend to fly without knowing that gravity exists, and they cry without knowing where tears come from. That is the child's journey of discovering the world he or she was placed in. Eventually, the child turns into an adolescent and is forced to think about the future. Later, the adolescent becomes an adult and has to deal with what once was only a vague notion of the future. That's when we begin to ask the big questions. *Who am I? Where do we come from?*

Who will I be? What is my purpose? It's a wonderful, personal, and confusing journey all at once—to know that one is alive for a purpose yet not knowing what it is can be challenging.

As a young adult, I often confused what I wanted my vocation to be with my purpose. A career or skill is an avenue for making a living, but it can be completely separate from one's life purpose. If we're lucky, our careers run parallel to our purpose. In my case, I always knew I wanted to be an artist, even when I believed I was the least talented in my family. Still, I felt a need to express myself at a young age. One can learn a set of skills, but I believe my passion and purpose were God-given, even before my birth. Eventually, everything came full circle, and one day it hit me. I began to cry. I finally understood my purpose, my reason for being alive. Without realizing that it was the silver lining of everything I did, everything I was drawn to since I was a child. It influenced the way I reacted to people and was the reason that certain stories affected my heart. It was the silent ache in my chest when I felt helpless to give aid to others. Then I understood that my purpose was my contribution to humanity. How was I contributing to my surroundings, to my people—inspiring other souls to find their purpose too?

I cannot be anyone's arteries, lungs, or liver, but I will share every part of myself if that helps just one person understand how their parts function too. I began to understand what my purpose was the moment I became more selfless because true purpose is rooted in helping others spiritually, mentally, or physically. It is a higher calling that exalts more than the self. *My purpose is my gift to the world; it is my contribution to someone's personal and spiritual growth.* Some days it may look small, but size doesn't matter when everyone's purpose serves a much larger kingdom.

The muse varies in creation,
but what doesn't vary is the origin of
    the muse.

The *must* feeling in creation
is the light that springs from the desire
    to create.

To bring forth to life
that which expresses an innate personal
    truth.

Attach yourself to your truth,
in order to listen to your muse.

The advice I give myself

I don't hear words
the way most people do.
I hear them with deep breaths,
music, laughter, and tears.
My mind is constantly
falling in and out of love,
creating and breaking,
living and feeling,
surviving only through
the mercy of *words*.

How my mind functions

17"

A stranger approached me and said
I had a fire within,
and I should never let it die.
He spoke confidently,
without knowing that
I was incapable of putting it out.
I smiled at him because I knew
that I was born an arsonist,
boldly spreading my light.

The habit of setting everything I love
on fire

When the muse arrives
and interrupts the pleasure
or the pain of my days,
I must stop
and give her my undivided attention.
Because if she leaves,
her words might not return again.

I am simply a vessel.

17

What is purpose?

Don't fret,
we all have one.
Yet it takes time
to see it clearly.

Mine is to uplift with love,
to restore the broken,
with the power of my words.

18"

What do I do?
I love.
What do I strive for?
A pure soul.

Love

One day I found myself meditating in solitude, and I felt a glorious presence come over me. My eyes watered from the peace and joy I felt. It was a warm and protective energy. I heard a voice whisper in my ear the following words, which I immediately wrote down.

To love is not to question but just to be. To be in the presence of light and be immersed in it. Allow that light to fill you even when you never sought it out. That is how love happens. It takes over without questions or answers. No one can know love unless he absolutely lets it happen, for control is part of the human ego. There is no ego in love. There is only freedom. When there is love, you will give naturally.

I can't describe exactly what happened in that moment, but I can confirm the amount of peace I felt. How true those words are. Every inch of my journey up to now has brought me to love. I have seen its many faces and its balance, because love is everywhere and everything derives from it. Love is simply the greatest gift of all.

If our lives were a script and each scene had an objective, every objective would relate to love. The reason we do the things we do is always rooted in love—the desire for it, the need for it, the lack of it, the willingness to give or to receive it.

It doesn't matter where in the world you were born or what socioeconomic class you were born into; we were all created to experience love. The time line of our experience can vary, but we were all born to walk with love. Every type of love has a meaningful value, whether it is romantic, familial, pragmatic, or agape. Unconditional love is the most difficult task for any human being to achieve because of the selflessness it requires. With or without our consent, life will constantly test the love within us, pushing us through the barriers of human conflict, enabling us to grow in wisdom or leaving us torn. It's as if the resolution to all our decisions, to everything at stake in the world, is and has always been based on love.

Every turn in my life has brought me to choose between two paths, one of light or one of darkness. If I'm touched by love, which is the light of the world, how can I ever choose a path of darkness? I don't need to remind myself of my character defects; that will only serve as an excuse to deny the person I was created to be. In order to excuse my shortcomings, many times I have said to myself, "I am only human." Yet I am a human being with knowledge of love and how to love. Because I have this knowledge and understand the power of love, I must choose accordingly. Each day I must choose to walk in a path of love. I must allow love to show me its many faces—its kindness, its empathy, its patience, its gratitude, its truth, and its forgiveness. I decided I must continue to push forward despite the disappointments, losses, and pains life's journey will bring. I choose love, and I will allow anything that springs from my life to be a testament to that love. It is a love that has the power to change the human heart and engage the human spirit; it possesses the strength to influence and renew the human mind.

Since an early age, I have prioritized romantic, passionate love, the "we can't live without each other" type of love. Although I still deeply desire to experience love like that again, I understand that the truth and wisdom of a universal love supersedes all other types. It's as if all the variations are the fruits of one specific tree, and for many years I only tasted several of those fruits but never fully understood the tree on which they grew. When I became more desirous of personifying unconditional love, an incredible amount of peace came into my life. That's when I learned to surrender to the creator's love—a perfect love in which fear does not abide. It is the love that can truly change the world and its inhabitants for the better; love is all we need.

We are all beings connected to that fruitful tree of life. We were all made with love by an all-loving creator. When I chose to walk in love, all I was doing was returning to my original nature. When I chose to walk in fear, I was returning to my original sin. Walking in love meant I had to learn how to love and forgive myself, to see myself with the same loving eyes the creator sees me with. I also had to express that love to others, and be a witness to it. If I deeply love someone, I will consciously not hurt them. I will consider their feelings as if they were my own. If I choose to not hurt someone because I'm afraid of the consequences, then real love never existed in the first place—fear did.

We feel with our hearts, and we think with our minds. But what of our soul? At times the heart can be deceiving, and the mind can be easily fooled—only the soul can navigate between both. The soul is the divine connection to the creator. When my spirit is strong, I am able to achieve more balance in my life. My heart can speak to me, inspire me, yet it speaks for my flesh. My mind can seek control and order, yet it speaks for the self. On the other hand, my soul speaks for my cumulative essence, an essence that is connected to the divine. It is all the beauty, peace, and things we hope for. *It speaks for its home, one that I yearn for.*

Love is the resurgence of memories
    every day.
Once those memories fade,
the love will begin to subside.
I hope you resurge in me the rest of
    my days.
I don't want to forget
your eyes and how they look at me,
your strong arms cocooning my body,
your half smile you love to hide,
and the way you run your fingers
through my hair.
Resurge in me
like deep ocean waters in a storm.
Resurge in me
like the burning fire of a thousand suns.

Resurge in me.

When I'm asked about him,
I immediately think of his
 unconventional face.
His arrogant nose
that painted my body like a brush.
His crooked smile
that lifted my spirits.
His deep eyes that made me weak
 with terror,
a terror only gods can comprehend,
because he was my thunder.
He was my war,
my calm,
the muse of my poetry,
the climax of my joy.

Meetings and encounters
are all designed to propel us
to higher levels of understanding.
When you came into my life
I didn't know the outcome.
I only knew that when I felt lost
you gave me hope.
You gave me words
when I lacked them.
You gave to me
what others took from me.
I now understand
it was love.

Encounters

18

I have loved before you
and confident as you are,
I hope your ego doesn't blind you.
I understand many men secretly wish
to be a woman's only love.
Yet in my story life took me on a
     different path,
and the world had to pluck me first.
Every love story is different,
and my stories are now shadows of
     my past.
So yes, I am unable to offer you many
     firsts,
but I can promise you my best love
because it's been broken and restored.
It has fallen and it has risen.
It has been pressured and now it shines.
It has walked on broken glass and
     endured.
That journey has brought me to
     your soul.
So yes, I have loved before you,
but none compares to you.
You are far better than my first
because you are my once-in-a-lifetime
     perfect love.

Promises to my future husband

I love to see
      people in love.
It doesn't matter the race
      or gender.
I love
      to see people care
for each other.
Maybe I love people
      or maybe I'm simply in love
with love.

In love with love

18″

How do I want to feel?

I want to be adored
and I want to feel safe.
I want someone who feels
our hearts were forged the same.

I am a woman who constantly wants
to defy gravity and the theory of time.
That is why I want you to look at me
the way you looked at me tonight.
I want your glance
to burn through me,
touch my insides
with your sight.
Tell me all the truths a man like you
has imprinted in his soul
and in his mind.
Hold my hand without deceit
and give me hours, minutes,
seconds I can't replace.
Hold me.
Don't attempt to read my mind,
simply hold me.

My plea to feel loved

When I was a child,
I acted like a child.
Now that I'm a woman in love,
how do you expect me to hide my smile?

When I fell in love

I can share my feelings with you,
but if you paid attention
to how I look at you,
you would know it all.

When my soul recognized you

So *this is how you fall in love.*
You close your eyes
and learn to dive in blindly.

To know love,
one must first
choose *to be love.*

Listen to your soul,
it always knows
where you should be.

When you seek, you will find.

Andrews McMeel Publishing
a division of Andrews McMeel Universal
1130 Walnut Street, Kansas City, Missouri 64106

www.andrewsmcmeel.com

20 21 22 23 24 BVG 10 9 8 7 6 5 4 3 2 1

ISBN: 978-1-5248-5832-2

Library of Congress Control Number: 2019956767

Editor: Patty Rice
Art Director/Designer: Julie Barnes
Production Editor: Amy Strassner
Production Manager: Cliff Koehler

FSC
www.fsc.org
MIX
Paper from
responsible sources
FSC® C102091

ATTENTION: SCHOOLS AND BUSINESSES
Andrews McMeel books are available at quantity discounts with bulk purchase for educational, business, or sales promotional use. For information, please e-mail the Andrews McMeel Publishing Special Sales Department: specialsales@amuniversal.com.